OCEAN VIEW

OCEAN VIEW

looking to the horizon

Perceptual Spaces

DEDICATION

This Book is Dedicated to Assateague Island National Seashore and all those who spend time maintaining and caring for this natural space.

Assateague Island spans 37 miles from Maryland to Virginia and runs along the eastern Atlantic coast of the Delmarva Peninsula. The Island is well known for its feral horses, lighthouse, and pristine beaches. Assateague is a wildlife refuge home to its ever-changing sandy beaches, salt marshes, coastal bays, and maritime forests.

CONTENTS

INTRODUCTION

All humans innately understand that nature has a powerful and mysterious attraction. Most humans can appreciate a sunrise or sunset, clouds moving across the sky, waves crashing on a beach, or watching wildlife interact with the environment. Nature is all around; it touches everything and is in everything humans create. Nature provides humans with food, all the raw or synthetic materials for shelter, and new technologies that are needed to survive and thrive throughout a lifetime.

This book is not a guide or how-to book. The intention was to create an experience by capturing nature via sight through imagery and language. In this book, perceptual spaces hopes to have captured and expressed, however small, the essence of the ocean.

There were many iterations as the book expanded and contracted several times, but, in the end, a condensed version emerged to quiet the feelings for simplicity. The overarching objective was to create something that would allow a person to spend time away from technology, reflect, let the mind breathe, or bring a person into the moment or a moment in time.

"Behold the Sea, The opaline, the plentiful and strong, Yet beautiful as is the rose in June,Fresh as the trickling rainbow of July; Sea full of food, the nourisher of kinds, Purger of earth, and medicine of men; Creating a sweet climate by my breath, Washing out harms and griefs from memory, And, in my mathematic ebb and flow, Giving a hint of that which changes not."

-Ralph Waldo Emerson

THE MIGHTY OCEAN

The English word ocean comes from the Old French word occean, which means a large body of water. Occean had a transition period between old french and modern English as occyan during the years 1100-1500.[1] But the French borrowed the word from the Latin langue oceanus, and the Romans adopted it from the Greek's ōkeanos. Oceanus was a Greek titan who was the son of the primordial gods Uranus which means sky, and Gaia, which means earth. The earth and sky united to create the vast ōkeanos, "the great river or sea surrounding the disk of the earth."[2] [3]

The ocean wraps the circumference of the earth, creating the largest interconnected body of water known in the universe. If Mt Everest were submerged in the deepest part of the ocean, the ocean would tower over Everest by more than a mile. All of the ocean's water could fill a tub that is 685 miles long and 685 miles wide. The five saltwater giants cover approximately 70 percent of the earth and makeup 97 percent of all water globally. The ocean is so vast that humans have explored only 5-10 percent of it. The sea is also home to a diverse set of saltwater aquatic species. Many oceanographers believe that 90 percent of these species are still undiscovered. These boundless bodies of water directly affect food supply, weather patterns, and temperature changes.[4] [5] [6]

Long before the oceans rose from the depths of the ethos, the earth was in its early stages of life and transformation. Around 4.6 billion years ago, the world was highly volatile during the Hadean Eon. The Hadean period was named after Hades and, in Greek, means "the underworld." During this epoch, the earth was a toxic hellscape. The world revolved at extreme speeds. Asteroids and space debris crashed into the planet, making it more unpredictable and erratic. This produced unusual weather patterns, a biosphere filled with toxic gases, seas of lava, and rivers of metal.[7] [8] [9]

Many believe the earth's ocean formed after the Theia impact. Theia was a giant planet or an asteroid the size of mars that collided with earth. The impact tilted the earth and produced space debris that got caught in the earth's gravitational pull. Over time the space debris that remained formed into the large entity humans call the moon. As the moon formed, the earth's rotation slowed, stabilizing and dropping its core temperature. This shift cooled the molten surface of the land and produced a gas that rose from the depths of the planet. This vapor cooled the earth and created the protective ozone layer that covers the world. This protective layer allowed the steam in the atmosphere to condense. Over time these gases, along with icy comets from space, formed the ocean some 3.8 billion years ago.[7][8][9]

The sea is an untamable space with relentless storms and unpredictable weather patterns. It is vast and home to the largest organisms in the world. The sea is a world unto itself and the most unexplored place on the planet. The ocean flows within all humans with mineral salts that regulate and balance the pressures of life.

Many mythologies, elaborate stories, monsters, gods, and metaphors have come from man's deep connection to the ocean. When humans gaze upon the ocean, they see the unknown. This mystery of the novel will always intrigue the human mind. It keeps humans moving forward in pursuit of touching new frontiers and capturing the essence of the ocean's horizon.

"Just as the wave cannot exist for itself, but is ever a part of the heaving surface of the ocean, o must I never live my life for itself, but always in the experience which is going on around me."

-Albert Schweitzer

REFERENCES

1. Ocean word origin [Internet]. Etymologeek. [cited 2022 Nov 10]. Available from: https://etymologeek.com/eng/ocean

2. Ocean [Internet]. Etymonline.com. [cited 2022 Nov 10]. Available from: https://www.etymonline.com/word/Ocean

3. Wikipedia contributors. Titans [Internet]. Wikipedia, The Free Encyclopedia. 2022. Available from: https://en.wikipedia.org/w/index.php?title=Titans&oldid=1120046772

4. The world ocean [Internet]. Nationalgeographic.org. [cited 2022 Nov 10]. Available from: https: education.nationalgeographic.org/resource world-ocean

5. Tech Insider. This incredible animation shows how deep the ocean really is [Internet]. Youtube; 2017 [cited 2022 Nov 10]. Available from: https: www.youtube.com/watch?v=UwVNkfCov1k

6. What is the mid-ocean ridge?: Ocean Exploration Facts: NOAA Ocean Exploration. 2014 [cited 2022   Nov 10]; Available from: https://oceanexplorer.noaa.gov/facts/mid-ocean-ridge.html

7. Walsh E. History of life on Earth [Internet]. Sciencing. Leaf Group; 2020 [cited 2022 Nov 10]. Available from: https://sciencing.com/evolution/

8. Hocken V. Earth is tilted [Internet]. Timeanddate.com. [cited 2022 Nov 10]. Available from: https://www.timeanddate.com/astronomy/axial-tilt-obliquity.html

9. Peshin A. How was the Earth formed? [Internet]. Science ABC. 2017 [cited 2022 Nov 10]. Available from: https://www.scienceabc.com/nature/universe/how-was-the-earth-formed.html

PERCEPTUAL SPACES

The outdoors has a profound way of bringing one into the moment, whether through the beauty of a landscape, standing under a waterfall, inhaling the sweet scent blowing in the wind, eating wild berries fresh from the land, or being subdued by the melodies of the forest. Nature has a way of creating a buffer between stressful events by contributing to one's mental, emotional as well as spiritual, and physical well-being.

Perceptual Spaces aims to create pieces that aid individuals on their journey toward decreasing stress and increasing overall well-being through content for the mind-body complex. Perceptual Spaces strives to inspire those who connect with our content to go and experience the majestic elements nature has to offer the senses.

CONNECT WITH PERCEPTUAL SPACES

Instagram

YouTube

TikTok

THANK YOU!

If you enjoyed this book, please leave a review on Amazon.

Relax • Focus • Meditate • Rest

© perceptual spaces 2022